John Moore Capes, Alfred Capes

The Old and New Churches of London

Being a Series of Illustrations of the Existing Remains of Church...

John Moore Capes, Alfred Capes

The Old and New Churches of London
Being a Series of Illustrations of the Existing Remains of Church...

ISBN/EAN: 9783337002954

Printed in Europe, USA, Canada, Australia, Japan

Cover: Foto ©ninafisch / pixelio.de

More available books at **www.hansebooks.com**

THE
OLD AND NEW
Churches of London

BEING A SERIES OF

ILLUSTRATIONS OF THE EXISTING REMAINS OF CHURCH ARCHITECTURE IN
LONDON FROM THE NORMAN PERIOD TO THAT OF THE GREAT FIRE

WITH NUMEROUS EXAMPLES OF THE

CHURCHES BUILT FROM THE YEAR 1844 TO THE PRESENT TIME

COLLECTED AND ARRANGED BY

ALFRED CAPES

ARCHITECT

With an Introductory Essay on the Principles of Architectural Beauty

BY THE

REV. J. M. CAPES, M.A.

LONDON
J. BUMPUS, 158 OXFORD STREET
OXFORD: SHRIMPTON & SON
1880

All rights reserved

LIST OF ILLUSTRATIONS.

			PLATE
St. Mary Overy.	(*Exterior*)	(*Frontispiece*)	1
Temple Church			2
Church of the Austin Friars.	(*Exterior*)		3
Church of the Austin Friars.	(*Interior*)		4
St. Etheldreda			5
St. Etheldreda.	(*Crypt*)		6
St. Mary Overy.	(*Lady Chapel*)		7
Chapel in the White Tower			8
Bow Church, Cheapside.	(*Crypt*)		9
Lambeth Palace.	(*Crypt*)		10
St. Stephen, Westminster			11
Lambeth Palace Chapel			12
St. Mary Aldermary.	(*Tower*)		13
St. Mary Aldermary.	(*Interior*)		14
St. Stephen, Walbrook			15
Stratford-le-Bow			16
St. Dunstan, Stepney			17

LIST OF ILLUSTRATIONS.

NEW CHURCHES.

		PLATE
St. Giles, Camberwell		18
All Saints, Margaret Street		19
St. Columba, Kingsland Road.	(*Exterior*)	20
St. Columba, Kingsland Road.	(*Interior*)	21
St. Stephen, Paddington		22
St. Mary Abbot, Kensington.	(*Exterior*)	23
St. Mary Abbot, Kensington.	(*Interior*)	24
St. Mary, Pimlico.	(*Exterior*)	25
St. Mary, Pimlico.	(*Interior*)	26
St. Jude, South Kensington.	(*Exterior*)	27
St. Jude, South Kensington.	(*Interior*)	28
St. Jude, Kensal Green		29
St. Chad, Haggerstone		30
St. Augustine, Kilburn		31
St. Mary, Stoke Newington		32
St. James-the-Less, Westminster		33
St. Saviour, Oxford Street		34
St. Gabriel, Pimlico		35
St. John Baptist, Kensington		36

THE OLD AND NEW CHURCHES
OF
LONDON.

THE PRINCIPLES OF ARCHITECTURAL BEAUTY.

1. 'ARE there really any principles of architectural beauty?' will be the first question asked by many people when they read the above heading.

'There are beautiful buildings,' they will say, 'and there are ugly buildings; just as there are beautiful faces and ugly faces. But does there exist any element in the nature of men and women on which can be based anything which can be called principle? any such universal agreement as to that which constitutes beauty, that we may study it scientifically, and on our scientific knowledge devise such an art, with its own special regulations, as will without doubt give pleasure to every sensitive and cultivated understanding?'

2. If such a principle exists, its application cannot be confined to architecture alone. Wherever the idea of beauty, as such, can exist, even in its humblest forms, this same principle must more or less be its life-giving element, down to what may be thought the trivialities of dress, or to such small matters

as can scarcely admit of any higher idea than that of mere prettiness and pleasantness of aspect.

3. The theory that this same feeling of beauty is the mere result of association, or of some artificial union between certain forms and certain ideas, will not stand a moment's serious examination. It is, nevertheless, a notion often to be met with. In the vehemence of religious controversies such notions sometimes assume an almost ludicrous aspect. Some years ago, it used to be seriously maintained that there was an essential fitness in the Gothic styles of the thirteenth and fourteenth centuries, to symbolise the action of the soul in divine prayer and praise. In the spire and the pointed arch, she found herself as it were at home, and in their upward tendencies she was aided in her struggles to escape from the pressure of earthly labours and earthly desires. The general adoption of Italian Architecture by Continental nations in their churches was counted as a sign of the corrupt character of the Modern Roman Theology. On the other hand, the passion for the Gothic styles which is so nearly universal among Englishmen of all schools and denominations, is to this day regarded by many foreigners as one of those peculiarities of the English nature which make the Englishman so strange and unaccountable a creature. The Englishman, moreover, of the very narrowest type would find a consolation in reflecting that Rickman, who with all his devotion to Gothic art was a Quaker, could never design a good Anglican church : and that the Roman Catholic Viollet-le-Duc, unrivalled in his knowledge of mediæval art and as a draughtsman, failed in his own architectural work.

4. Then, again, architectural beauty is often said to be a

result of the harmonious relations of its various parts, and I have heard a great cathedral described as music transformed into stone. Here the ingenious speaker simply meant that the cathedral affected him as a superb piece of music affected him. He did not see that he was supplying no answer to the question why the cathedral any more than the symphony moved him so profoundly, perhaps even to tears. So, further, we are told that the secret of architectural beauty lies in proportion. But what is proportion ? Whatever be the essence of the idea itself, it is perhaps more difficult to define it in itself than to illustrate it by examples of its opposites. As an example of disproportion in a flagrant degree, I may specify the size of many of the sculptured figures in St. Peter's at Rome. These are for the most part far above the ordinary height of man, and are therefore absolutely out of proportion to the building in which they are placed, which is designed for human use. They reach their climax of artistic absurdity in the huge *baldacchino*, or canopy, under the dome, where four giants in fluttering garments hold up by their fingers a vast, shapeless roofing, strikingly resembling the top of a four-post bedstead, over what is called the 'Tomb of the Apostles.' Nor need I be deterred by the great name of Michael Angelo from describing his wonderful Prophets and Sybils in the roof of the Sistine Chapel as out of proportion to the chapel itself, or from saying the same of his still more marvellous figures of the two Medici and of Night and Morning at Florence.

5. Every colossal figure which is placed in a building occupied by human beings is in truth out of proportion to the building itself. The same fault is to be found with colossal

figures out of doors when they are combined with figures of a lesser size, unless there is some special meaning expressed by their gigantic magnitude, as was the case with many of the sculptures of ancient Greece, where colossal size was designed to symbolise divinity. This is why the enormous bigness of the principal figure in the Albert Memorial is universally felt to be a mistake. The accompanying Allegorical and Portrait groups at the four corners prove that the art of sculpture is a living art amongst us. But the Prince, whose glory they are supposed to set forth, was not a demi-god among mortals.

Once more, if any man wishes to learn how the idea of proportion may be cast to the winds in such simple matters as doors, windows, pillars, and pilasters, let him look up Regent Street, and survey that masterpiece of architectural ugliness. Here he shall see what could be done when the 'genius' of Nash was inspired by the wishes of George IV.; and house fronts which seemed to have been sketched by the daring pencil of an upholsterer were executed with an unlimited profusion of cement and plaster.

6. Besides, whatever may be the meaning with which we use the term proportion, it is certainly not the same thing as beauty. It is not that secret power which awakens in the cultivated and sensitive mind a mysterious sense of enchantment, as if it were in the presence of some hidden power, which lived a life of its own beyond the reach of all the rules and regulations of art and the deductions of science. Beauty in architecture, then, is the result not only of the adoption of certain curves and straight lines, accompanied with a suggestion of structural strength and of practical adaptation to the purposes for which the building is

raised, but upon the more or less frequent repetition of some unit of length, which seizes upon the eye of the spectator, and fills his mind with a sense of harmony of which he is none the less conscious because he cannot explain precisely what it is that he feels. Upon this skeleton or linear structure the designer proceeds to place a multitude of details, in themselves suggestive of fitness and utility, and in their combination pleasant and varied. Taken singly, the effect of these essentials will not amount to positive beauty, though there can be no beauty without them. For I use the word beauty in its strictest sense, as expressing the highest perfection which man's art can attain.

7. It is in the same way that the idea of beauty attaches to other results of men's genius, and the face and figure of man himself. There are multitudes of women with charming faces, but there are few of whom it can be said that they are beautiful. Gibson, one of the most accomplished of sculptors and acutest and fairest of critics, once said that in all his experience he had only seen one person whose face and figure were without defect, and that was a Roman boy, who at the time he said this was in prison for stabbing his brother.

So it is in music and poetry. There are innumerable compositions and poems delightful to hear or read; but there are not many that rise to the height of the absolutely beautiful. As an instance of musical beauty on a grand scale, I may specify the concluding chorus in Bach's 'Matthæus Passion,' and on a smaller scale Mozart's 'Ave Verum Corpus.' Among Beethoven's masterpieces the Adagio in his posthumous Quartett in B flat is a movement which to the understanding ear is entrancing in its beauty. Among well-known poems, Shelley's 'Ode to a Skylark' is beautiful to perfection, and Tennyson has written a few songs and short poems which are as beautiful as a Greek statue.

8. Returning to our main subject, there can be no doubt that it is in the adoption of some prominent unit, and in its repetition more or less strict, including divisions of the same, that the highest beauty in architecture can alone be reached. And this natural law, for it is a law, which is dependent upon some universal element in our nature, prevails alike in the Gothic and the Italian (in which I include the Roman) forms. In the best Italian works it appears in the division of the exterior (implying a corresponding division of the interior) into stages, or floors of exactly equal heights, the projecting lines of the different cornices thus catching the eye of the spectator and compelling him to regard the building as a whole, and not as a mere pile of rooms, in which the sentiment of pettiness and shabbiness interferes with the effect of the cleverness, or even excellence, of some of the details. Of this fundamental conception in architectural design, the Banqueting Hall, at Whitehall, now a chapel royal, is the most familiar to Londoners among Italian works. And this adoption of stories of equal height runs throughout the whole of Inigo Jones's design for the vast palace which was to be raised for the Stuarts, and which would have given to the English Monarchy the very biggest palace, save the Spanish Escurial, in which Europe lodged the Absolutism of the past. Intelligent criticism observes at a glance that it is this marked division of the design into two portions of equal height which gives its dignity to that which is a mere fragment, and which tells the passer by that he is standing beneath the work of one of the great masters of the architectural art.

9. Not far from this fragment of the home of absolutism stands that other palace, which the popular sovereignty of modern days has raised to be the home of Legislative Freedom. The Houses of Parliament are the most magnificent single buildings that modern Europe has seen, and it is designed on identically the same theory as the Whitehall Banqueting Room. Its front is divided into two stories of equal height, and the same theory prevails throughout the building. The whole design of the river front, notwithstanding the multiplicity of its details, is singularly broad and simple, and the result is a remarkable aspect of unity and repose. The immeasurable superiority of the Gothic forms over the Italian, as suitable for the towers and spires necessary to prevent the dulness inseparable from immense masses in any variety in Italianism, and which are so striking a feature in the Houses of Parliament, only serve to bring into clearer prominence the principle of repetition which is common to both styles.

10. Sir Charles Barry was in truth an architect of nothing less than genius, and his memory will not suffer if I ask attention to an example in which he violated the principle on which I am insisting, and in which he himself admitted that he had done wrong. His design for the Reform Club House, in Pall Mall, is manifestedly suggested by the Borghese Palace in Rome, as completed by Michael Angelo. But it is seriously injured by the lessening of the height of the third story, in comparison with those below. To the eye familiar with the great works, both of Italian and Gothic Architecture, the result is nothing less than painful.

11. How constantly this law of equal division and repetition prevails in the artistic works of such men as Michael Angelo, Raf-

facile, and Bramante, I need not remind the cultivated architect. But its importance was felt from the earliest times, when the old Roman style, having grown out of the old Greek, was preparing itself for a future development into that Italian modification which was required by the habits of modern life, and which we associate with the period of the Renaissance. In the floors of the Roman Coliseum the principle is rigidly observed, and notwithstanding the huge size of the building all sense of monstrosity and heaviness is thus obviated, and that sense of unity, lightness, and structural safety is secured, which we miss in more modern attempts at grandeur and dignity.

12. It is the same in the finest Gothic works of the thirteenth and fourteenth centuries, in which by universal consent the feeling of beauty is most successfully attained, in union with magnificence and greatness. Of this union there is no more striking instance than the Cathedral of Amiens. There we have a fixed unit of length, first adopted as a division in the pavement of the floor of the nave, then recurring exactly in itself or in one of its multiples in the height of the piers up to the springing of the arch, thence, again, to the strongly marked projecting line of moulding below the triforium; then, again, with more or less rigid exactness in the height of the clerestory, and again, with its arithmetical divisions throughout the building, both horizontally and perpendicularly. In London a specially suggestive illustration of the influence of this principle is to be seen in the beautiful church of St. Mary Overy, which was not very long ago chiefly known as St. Saviour's, Southwark, and the sight of whose rare beauty is now so grievously interfered with by a hideous railway. Who, indeed, can wonder at the Continental conviction,

that the English people love money, and nothing but money, when he sees one of the most precious legacies of mediæval art, which time, or rather the hand of unscrupulous men, has spared, now in this age of Art Education thus practically sacrificed to add a few pounds to the value of sundry railway shareholders in their lust for gain under the contagion of the madness of the hour? In St. Mary Overy the recognition of the principle is a little less rigid than at Amiens, but it has furnished the fundamental idea on which its architect drew the general outlines of his design, and it is especially manifest in the central tower (Frontispiece).

It is, too, in this unconscious sense of repetition, I may note before proceeding further, that we are satisfied, so to say, with the equilateral, above all other varieties of the pointed arch. Here we have the space between the bases of the two sides of the arch equal to a right line drawn from the springing to the point of the arch. So, further, in the round arch. Unless it is an exact semicircle in which the space between the points of the springing of the sides of the arch is exactly equal to twice the radius of the circle itself, we are unpleasantly impressed that as an arch the construction is faulty.

13. How deeply the desire for this systematic repetition is implanted in our nature is to be estimated from its prevalence in the human face and body itself. The recognition by nature of this principle of the repetition of the linear unit in the construction of the human frame is a fact which is noted by every authority who has studied the intimate connection which exists between beauty and structural laws. Those who doubt this connection are those who have not made it a matter of serious study.

In the human figure the unit is the height of the head, from the base of the chin to the top of the skull; and the height of the perfect figure is just eight times the height of the head. The head itself is again divided into two equal portions at the centre of the eyeballs; and similar divisions prevail throughout, from the chief division into two equal portions at the umbilical point down to the division of the hands and fingers. The circumferences of various parts of the body are, moreover, multiples of the circumference of one part; and generally, without being aware of it, it is by this means that when in the presence of the masterpieces of Greek sculpture we are enthralled by an indescribable sense of their beauty and their structural power.

This union of beauty and expressiveness with the physical force resulting from the disposition and size of the hidden bones and tendons within, is to be especially noted in the two great statues so well known to English people—the 'Apollo Belvedere' and the 'Dying Gladiator.' The expression of haughty delight with which the Apollo watches the flight of his death-bearing arrow is combined with an erectness of limb and a disposition of the arms so beautiful as to suggest a divinity within, and we almost forget that the entire figure is a masterpiece of constructive strength.

The 'Dying Gladiator' is, if possible, a still more instructive example of that sense of the beautiful which is created by the mere disposition and proportion of the various portions of the physical frame. Lord Byron's speculations as to the wanderings of the slaughtered Dacian's thoughts to his 'Young barbarians all at play,' by the waters of the distant Danube, are purely fictitious. No such thoughts are passing through the mind of the dying man. The real statue represents simply the final conflict between physical life and death. The heart is about to cease to beat, and it is through the sustaining physiological power resulting from a perfectly knit anatomical structure that the dying man still 'leans upon his hand,' and is not already prostrate upon the earth. There is no thought or emotion left upon the all but lifeless countenance. It is a masterpiece of pathos and power, but it is thus sad and powerful because it tells of the all-conquering death, and which makes us feel all the more keenly the exquisite beauty of the limbs, thus on the point of yielding to their last destroyer.

14. Between the application of this fundamental element of beauty in architecture and its application by the hand of nature, there is, indeed, one important distinction. In every work of man, from the most magnificent cathedral down to the humblest piece of furniture, we are compelled to follow the strict rule of symmetry, almost universally, either in our complete structure or in its details. In nature such strict symmetry is absolutely unknown. The two sides of a trunk of a tree, its lateral branches and twigs, the sides of the leaves and buds of the trees and flowers—all these vary slightly in the corresponding portions. So, again, in the human face, body, and limbs—here strict symmetry is unknown. No man's two hands are exactly alike; and so with his arms, legs, and feet. An absolutely symmetrical face is never seen, except in the statues and paintings of modern artists. In no face do the two sides literally correspond. The eye alone is geometrically true, for unless both the eyeball and the iris, with the pupil, were perfectly circular, the functions of the organ could not be fulfilled.

15. It is, as I have said, from their ignorance of this unvarying absence of rigid symmetry that the ideal sculpture and painting of the modern artist are so destitute of life and meaning. Not so with the Greeks. In the Elgin Marbles themselves may be seen an illustration of their knowledge of the true facts of life; and hence, among other causes, the wonderful sense of vitality with which those marbles impress us. But I know no antique bust in which this absence of rigid symmetry is so bold and impressive as it is in the superb colossal head known as the Giustiniani Apollo, at the British Museum. Here the two sides of the mouth are so unlike that the expression of the face when looked at on one side is actually contradictory to that of the other. Yet the whole head is splendidly beautiful.

16. That the laws of Gothic Architecture allow greater freedom in this respect than is permitted by those of Italian, and still more than is possible in the pure Greek, architecture, is not to be denied. And there was a period in our modern English 'Gothic revival' when a sort of disorderliness of design was accounted a characteristic of the true Gothic. This misconception is fast dying out, though it is not everywhere dead. Our best architects have long learnt that where Gothic architecture is irregular it is for some definite reason of structure or practical utility. Windows and doorways sprawling about the outside of a building, with turrets, pinnacles, and gables *ad libitum*, added for the sake of the 'picturesque,' no more produce the spirit of mediæval art than does the self-satisfied haughtiness of the prize-winner in a country archery fête suggest the godlike scorn and joy of the Apollo Belvedere.

17. There exists, indeed, in all sensitive minds an undeniable

desire for the introduction of this free life of Nature into the formal rigidity of architectural structure. Freedom from hard symmetry is the sign of the presence of that mysterious life in the firmament and on earth from which they derive their beauty. From the love of what is called 'real lace,' in whose network there is no precise symmetry upwards, we enjoy the sight of that freedom of the hand which implies the work of a living artist and workman. What is called 'formality' is an objection everywhere.

18. And here I may note that in its period of highest brilliancy Gothic architecture attained a power of introducing this freedom which is everywhere else unattainable. In her works of the fourteenth century, known as the Flowing Decorated, the tracery of her windows is often drawn, not by measurements with a pair of compasses, but by the untrammelled hand of the architect. Hence the corresponding curves in a window do not always correspond with one another with strict precision; and we feel as if the lovely grouping of graceful forms grew into being, rather than were carved by the hand of some careful stone-cutting mechanic.

19. Here, too, I will venture to offer to the reader a view as to the essence of the life of pointed architecture which is not in accordance with the popular theory. Surely it is the window far more than in the pointed arch that the works of the latter end of the thirteenth century, and all those of the fourteenth, are what they are. Without the aid of the pointed arch, it is true, the window tracery, which is the glory of Gothic art, could not have been invented. The single one-light windows could not have been tied together, and the intervening spaces of their upper

parts been filled with tracery, under a round arch. And this it has proved in reality. In Italian architecture, the window, as such, is a mere opening in the wall. As an element in the structural beauty of the church or the palace it has no existence. Give it what beauty we may with pediments, lateral columns, and mouldings, in itself it is a large opening and nothing more, like the dull fishy eyes of a man or woman who can neither think nor feel.

20. Various guesses have been made as to the origin of the pointed arch and the date of its introduction into Europe. But, let me ask, where would Gothic Architecture have been but for the introduction of window glass at a comparative cheap cost and in practically sufficient quantities in the thirteenth century? It was the sudden placing at the architect's disposal of all the brilliant light which sparkles through the coloured medium of the fourteenth-century glass which stimulated the mind to invent those marvels of beauty and brightness in which after-ages delight, but which they do not rival. The window, in truth, as such, from the very first, even before the introduction of tracery, seems to have exercised a special influence in pointed architecture. The simple lancet was instantly found to be capable of imparting a peculiar sense of repose and harmony, until its charm was superseded by the more brilliant attractiveness of the succeeding date.

In England there remain some of the most faultless examples of this purest and sweetest of all architectural forms. And in no city of Europe are to be found two such delightful illustrations of the principles on which I have been insisting as are supplied by St. Mary Overy and the Temple Church (Plate 2).

To judge of the means, or artifice, so to say, by which these two churches attain their beauty, they must be studied in their 'elevations' on paper and not merely in perspective views. Here we have a perfect refinement and delicacy of outline, and that knitting together of curves and straight lines which create that indescribable sense of repose and dignity which appears in its noblest development in the famous transept at York and in Beverley Minster. This, too, is the most difficult of all pointed styles to the modern architect, just as it is so difficult to the sculptor to approach the calm dignity of the antique Aristides at Naples, or the modern Houdin's St. Bernard at Rome, of which it was said by the wittiest of all Popes, Benedict XIV., that 'he would speak, if the rule of his order did not forbid him.' St. Bernard was of the Cistercian order, which keeps a perpetual silence.

21. Of the capabilities of the Gothic window, both in the creation of tracery in itself and of its character when it seems to have grown into existence by a life of its own, the two most striking examples remaining in London have passed away from the possession of the Church of England. The Church of the Austin Friars (Plate 3) is now used for the services of the Dutch, whose religious offices are of the very simplest kind; while the Church of St. Etheldreda, in Ely Place, belongs to the Roman Catholics.

There are, perhaps, no more beautiful windows of the latter part of the fourteenth century than those in the Austin Friars (Plate 4), and in the hands of its present owners all possible care will be taken of the structure.[1] The story of its transfer

[1] It was not long ago carefully restored by Mr. Ianson.

to the Dutch is curious enough. It is to be found in the 'History of the French Wallons, Dutch, and other foreign refugees, by J. S. Burn.' From this rare book it appears that the Flemings, forming part of the body of strangers, were incorporated by Edward VI., and were settled as a congregation in Austin Friars by letters patent, dated July 24, 1550, where one John A'Lasco was appointed first superintendent. From the following notice in the Acta Regia, it would appear that they had been allowed to use the church of the Austin Friars nearly two hundred years, having taken sanctuary there in the rebellion of Wat Tyler in 1381, when many Flemings, as well as Englishmen, were executed. The story runs that thirteen Flemings were brought out of the Austin Friars church, seventeen out of another church, and thirty-two from the Vintry, all of whom were beheaded, unless they could distinctly pronounce the words *Bread and Cheese*, which the Flemings were apt to pronounce as *Brot and Cause*. Edward VI. also, in his diary for June 29, writes that it was appointed that the Germans should have the Austin Friars for their church, 'for avoiding all sects of Anabaptists and such like.'

In 1566, the King of Spain, having complained that his subjects of the Low Countries had been harboured in England, ordered Bishop Grindall to take their names, which was done by the minister. The superintendence of A'Lasco extended not only to the German congregation, but to all foreign churches in London, and their schools. He was a great friend of Erasmus, and was with him at his death, and became possessed of his library.

The Church of St. Etheldreda once formed part of the famous palace in Holborn. The large east and west windows are among the most characteristic and perfect examples of the early part of the fourteenth century to be found anywhere in England, and must have awakened new conceptions as to the possibilities of artistic beauty in the men who first saw them rise into life. Our engraving (Plate 5) represents the west window.[1] The crypt (Plate 6) itself is very singular, being built entirely of wood, probably with the intention of replacing the wood with the usual stone vaulting.

Of pointed vaulting when it had attained its highest perfection, though not its extreme enrichment, no examples can be named more beautiful than those at the Temple Church and St. Mary Overy (Plate 7).

22. Taking our other illustrations in chronological order, few of the dungeons of mediæval Europe are more pregnant with terrible associations than the Chapel of the White Tower, in the Tower of London (Plate 8). The architecture itself is a somewhat rude example of the early Norman, and the roof is of the simplest barrel form. The chapel is full of memories of the prisoners who lingered within those gloomy walls year after year, and here heard the hurried Masses which were said for them when the clergy were the chief defenders of the poor and suffering, against the rampant cruelties of feudalism.

23. Of the Norman roof in its groined form, and employed so as to carry the weight of a heavy structure, a pure and characteristic example is to be seen in the crypt under the east

---

[1] For the originals of this engraving, as well as that of the crypt of the same church, we are indebted to the liberality of the proprietors of the *Graphic*.

end of Bow Church, Cheapside (Plate 9). The engraving here is a copy from that which was taken from the excellent drawing made for the Society of Antiquaries by Mr. George Gwilt, and published by them in the 'Vetustæ Monumenta,' in 1835. Mr. Gwilt accompanied the engraving with some observations so interesting and important that I quote them as they stood. 'The walls of this crypt remain nearly entire. It is divided into three portions; the centre or nave is 48 feet 7 inches long from east to west, by 26 feet 7 inches wide. On either side extends an aisle or corridor the same length as the nave, by 14 feet 5 inches wide. The whole extent of this crypt covers a space 78 feet by 60 feet. Communications between each of the aisles and the nave are obtained by four lofty doorways on each side, each 4 feet wide. The walls, which are over 5 feet thick, are carried up to the springing line of the arches, in neat and regular courses of block and block masonry; above that line they are of rubble intermixed with Roman brick. The groined arches are mostly of an elliptic form, but those in the nave, which turn from north to south, are semicircles, somewhat elevated above the springing levels. It is observable that the foci of the ellipses in the nave, extending east and west, are fixed at a distance from the centre line or conjugate diameter of exactly one fourth of the opening or transverse diameter; *i.e.* the opening being divided into four parts, the foci are fixed upon the first and third divisions. This arrangement produces a well-proportioned and easy curve. The arches and ribs are turned with rubble masonry and Roman brick, and appeared to have been originally stuccoed or plastered over. Four windows may be distinctly braced in the most northern wall towards Cheapside, although they are now masoned up; and one at the end of the nave. Three of the columns, as shown in the plate, remain; the other three, with their superincumbent arches, have been removed. The columns which remain are destitute of decoration to their capitals, but they approach nearer to the lofty portions of the Lombardic style of the eleventh and twelfth centuries than generally occurs in similar buildings of that period in this country. As the greater part of the original church fell down in 1272, and was subsequently altogether destroyed, with the exception of the crypt, it may be some satisfaction to trace, if possible, the peculiar features of the construction of the crypt itself from the analogy of existing buildings. With this view I have compared it with that of St. Peter's at Oxford, commonly called Grymball's crypt, which seems to have been constructed on principles exceedingly similar to those at Bow Church. Of the former, the upper part of the building remains nearly entire, and the comparison may be made.

There can be indeed but little or no doubt that the upper part of Bow Church was a close approximation in style and character to the chancel at St. Peter's at Oxford, but it would be too much to assume that the pointed arch was also introduced in the way we find it made use of in the latter building; nor would it be so indispensably necessary at Bow Church, where the side aisles might be made available for the introduction of sufficient counteracting abutments, while on the other hand it will be obvious that the pointed arch was adopted at Oxford in preference to a semicircular, to diminish the lateral pressure upon walls without abutting piers or buttresses, and which after all have been unequal to the service they were destined to perform. Witness the crippled state of the south side wall. The introduction of the pointed arch in the circular style at a period so far removed (as in the example before us) would lead to offer' some observations on its much-contested origin; but as such would be foreign to the present occasion, I will not pursue the subject.'

24. Of the lighter forms of the arch when it had become pointed and the conception of the moulding as such was filling the minds of the thirteenth-century architects, we have an extremely interesting illustration of its underground use in the crypt at Lambeth Palace (Plate 10). The singular wooden crypt under the church of St. Etheldreda (Plate 5) is no doubt of about the same date of construction, while it was in all probability intended to last only until a stone vaulting could be set up in its place.

The crypt under the Houses of Parliament, named after St. Stephen (Plate 11), and now restored for the purposes of public worship, is probably as perfect an illustration of the vaulted roofing of a somewhat later date as is to be found either in England or on the Continent. The restoration under the late Mr. E. Barry from the designs of his father preserved to the nation the only remaining portion of the original palace of Westminster, and suggests the belief that the palace as it was originally raised in the fourteenth century was one of the finest pieces of Gothic Art in the world.

The chapel at Lambeth Palace (Plate 12) is a fair illustration of the character and beauty of the household ecclesiastical work which was common in the days when feudalism reigned triumphant, and the Archbishop of Canterbury was not only the head of the English Church, but the chief of its parliamentary magnates. There are many things full of the deepest historical interest about the Palace, but it is only the chapel and the crypt, to which we have already referred, which call for present illustration.

25. Of the roofs of the thirteenth and fourteenth centuries there are none more beautiful than those in the Temple Church and in St. Mary Overy (Plate 6). Of its latest development as fan-shaped, St. Mary Aldermary (Plates 13, 14)[1] furnished an illustration which is at once a proof of the capabilities of the style and of the extraordinary genius of Sir Christopher Wren. Here, indeed, the fan-shaped work is far from pure, but the church as a whole, taken in connection with Wren's masterpiece at St. Stephen's, Walbrook, and with the dome at St. Paul's, entitles him to a place among the great architects of all ages. A large portion of the church, which was originally built early in the sixteenth century, was destroyed in the great fire. It was rebuilt in the original style by Wren in 1682, and has lately been placed in its present perfect condition under the superintendence of Mr. C. Innes.

26. The design of St. Stephen's, Walbrook (Plate 15), deserves a somewhat detailed description, as there is no more beautiful church in its style and for its size in Europe. Outside, the church is ugly enough. In the interior, in four rows of Corinthian columns, within one intercolumniation from the east end, two columns from each of the two centre rows are omitted,

---

[1] For the original of this engraving, as well as that of the chapel in the White Tower, we are indebted to the liberality of the proprietors of the *Illustrated London News*.

and the area thus formed is covered by an enriched cupola, supported on eight arches which rise from the entablature of the columns.

27. With a brief reference to an important element in architectural beauty, which has been too long neglected, we may proceed to the necessary notices of the new churches, which the present generation has seen start into life all over London. Yet this element of beauty has been recognised by the great architects of all ages alike. They invariably make the lower portions of their buildings more simple and solid than the upper. Modern ignorance likes to see all the fine and expensive work down below, and near the eye. The laws of structure insist that inasmuch as the lower part of a building must necessarily carry a heavier burden than the higher, its windows shall be barely what convenience demands, and the entire stage or stages shall not be in reality, but evidently, simple and equal to all that is laid upon them.

Thus in the most perfect mediæval towers the highest stories are often actually more lofty than the lower, as well as being lighter in their design and details. And thus it is that it is usually easy to say at a moment's glance that an old Gothic church was unquestionably built before the Reformation from that unquestionable air of simplicity and utility which pervades it throughout. Even when there is nothing strikingly good about it, there is an absence of affectation and showiness which tells at once that its architect thought in Gothic, so to say, and that the days of competitions, exhibitions, academies, and revivalism were yet unknown. Two such churches are Stratford-le-Bow (Plate 16) and St. Dunstan, Stepney

(Plate 17). The former is the least important building of the two, but it has its special interest as the church whose bells sang 'Turn again, Whittington' in the ears of the future Lord Mayor of the legend, and the biggest of which peal is the 'Great Bell of Bow,' familiar to the children of England in the jingle about the 'Bells of London Town.' In this church we have a tower with a nave and chancel, in which, as is not usual with buildings of this date (about A.D. 1490), the roof has not been lowered in pitch. The east window is a really fine example of Perpendicular work; but throughout the whole there is not one single feature of which it could be said that the architect placed it where it is, for the sake of show, or in order to cause the beholder to remark that he was a very clever fellow.

St. Dunstan (Plate 17), Stepney, was built in the reign of Henry VI. or Edward IV. It has happily fallen into good hands, and in the present condition represents architecturally the continuity of the Anglican from the Roman Church, so far at least as its possessions are concerned.

28. Leaving Stratford and Stepney, however, I ought to add that our modern English fondness for making our buildings, domestic and religious, diminish in height and beauty in their higher stages, is one fruitful source of that failure to command admiration which is so frequent all over the land. From the numerous gentlemen's 'seats' which abound wherever the country landowners possess a few thousand acres, down to the London houses of all sizes and pretensions, the same air of paltriness and shabbiness pervades the higher stories. It is common enough to meet with large houses, or 'mansions,' as the cant of the day loves to term them, in which the highest

row of windows are even wider than they are high. Hence the utter want of dignity in the general street architecture of London. The feeling for simple loftiness, as such, seems strange to the genuine Briton. All that he has learnt of the spirit of true Italian architecture is its squareness.

At the same time the improvement in what I may call the tone of London house architecture, whenever a capable architect is engaged by a man of sense and good taste, is striking. The designs for work of all kinds which appear weekly in the three architectural journals bear evidence to this advance.[1] Only let me here venture to remind the lovers of the 'Queen Anne's Style,' which is now becoming popular, that strictly speaking it is no style at all, but an accidental Anglicised continuation of the brick-architecture imported into England by William III., who brought it from a country where there is little stone and timber, and where clay abounds. Furthermore, it is just as easy to build a very bad imitation of the 'Queen Anne Style' as a very bad imitation of the Gothic of the fourteenth century. The actual Queen Anne architects were free from the influence of the spirit of revivalism, and they built for use and not for oddity.

---

[1] The plan of the present work excludes everything of the nature of criticism of the modern churches illustrated, which are simply described in their several characteristics. But I cannot refrain from referring to a drawing of a country church in the *Building News*, March 15, 1878, as showing how great is the merit to which our modern architects are capable of attaining. It is the west elevation of a church at Horsham, rebuilt for the Rev. Canon Bridges by Mr. Brock. This elevation is really beautiful, and it is a pleasure to study it as a whole and in its details. The tower and spire are a marked proof of that principle of repetition to which I have called attention as the first element in architectural beauty. The four lower stages of the buttresses of the tower are exactly equal in height; the highest division in the tower itself is equal in height to the lowest stage in the spire; then follow two equal divisions in the spire. The eye is thus *satisfied*, and the mind is impressed with a sense of united strength, simplicity, and grace.

TEMPLE CHURCH.

CHURCH OF THE AUSTIN FRIARS.

CHURCH OF THE AUSTIN FRIARS.

ST ETHELDREDA ELY PLACE

CRYPT OF ST ETHELDREDA.

ST MARY OVERY LADY CHAPEL.

Plate 7

CHAPEL IN THE WHITE TOWER.

LAMBETH PALACE CHAPEL.

CRYPT — LAMBETH PALACE.

Plate II.   ST. STEPHEN'S CHAPEL, WESTMINSTER.

ST MARY ALDERMARY.

PLATE 14.

ST. MARY, ALDERMARY.

ST. STEPHEN, WALBROOK.

Plate 16.

STRATFORD-LE-BOW CHURCH

Plate 17

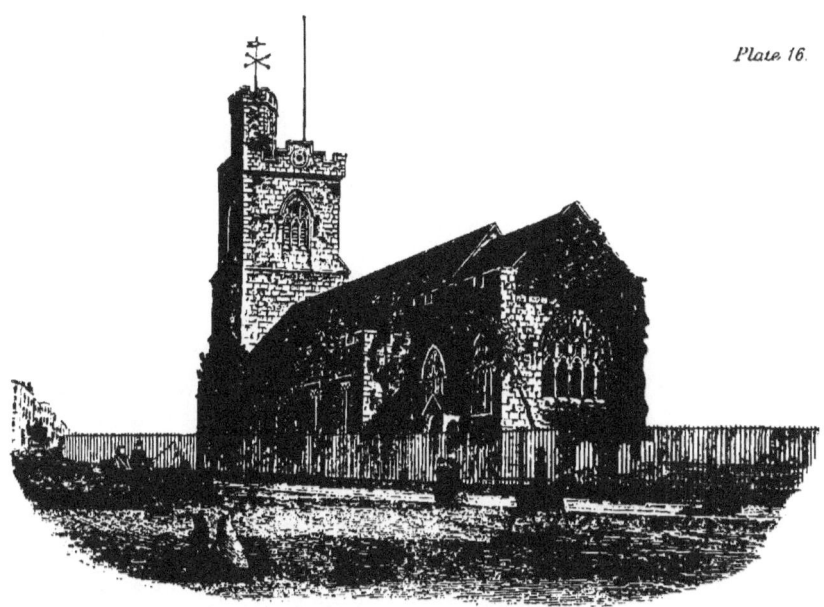

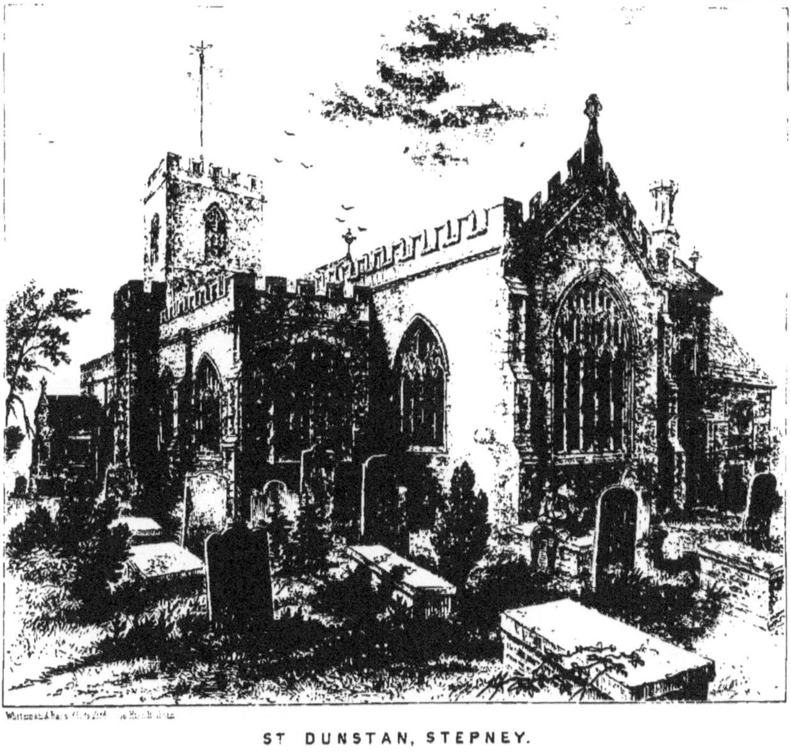

ST DUNSTAN, STEPNEY.

ST. GILES'S, CAMBERWELL.

ST. GILES'S CHURCH was one of the first buildings which brought the late Sir Gilbert Scott into general public notice. He was at that time in partnership with Mr. Moffatt; but the design of the church was due to Mr. Scott himself, who about the same time designed the very clever Martyrs' Memorial at Oxford, a building which excited the most opposite feelings in the different parties in the Church, but about whose merits, as a Memorial Cross, there was but one opinion. Old Camberwell Church was a tolerable specimen of the patched-up suburban buildings, of which few now remain, but it had a picturesque tower, and satisfied the desires of the people of the old school. The present building is in the style of the early part of the fourteenth century, and holds about 1,200 persons. The organ is by Bishop. Our illustration gives a very fair idea of the general character of the building, and shows how early Sir Gilbert Scott was entitled to claim that place among English church architects which was universally conceded to him. The present vicar is the Rev. F. F. Kelly.

ST. GILES' CHURCH, CAMBERWELL.

ALL SAINTS', MARGARET STREET.

ALL SAINTS' CHURCH, of which the Rev. Berdmore Compton is the vicar, is the successor to a small chapel which went by the name of Margaret Chapel, which was well known to the generation of church-goers now rapidly passing away. The present building was designed by Mr. Butterfield, with those disadvantages of cramped space which have hampered the skill of so many modern London architects. The church holds 700 people. The organ is by Hill and Sons.

ALL SAINTS, MARGARET STREET.

ST. COLUMBA'S, HAGGERSTON.

St. Columba's Church, of which the Rev. J. Vodin-Walters is the vicar, is an example of the architecture of a somewhat later period in the church-building movement. Its architect is Mr. J. Brooks; and the style, that commonly known as Early English. It is a large church, holding 1,000 people. The organ is by Allen, of Bristol. We are enabled to give an illustration both of its interior and exterior.

ST. STEPHEN'S, PADDINGTON.

In St. Stephen's Church, of which the Rev. T. J. Rowsell is the vicar, Messrs. F. and H. Francis, the architects, have had every advantage of space; and our engraving shows how well they have known how to take advantage of their situation. By the aid of galleries, which were no part of their original design, the church holds 1,600 persons. The windows are nearly all filled with stained glass. The organ is by Hill and Sons.

ST. STEPHEN'S CHURCH, WESTBOURNE PARK, PADDINGTON.

ST. MARY ABBOTT'S, KENSINGTON.

ST. MARY ABBOTT'S, the parish church of Kensington, was one of the last churches built by the late Sir Gilbert Scott; and it may be taken, in comparison with St. Giles's, Camberwell, as an illustration of the modification in his characteristic style, which was the result of the general church-building movement of the last forty years. It holds as many as 1,500 persons. The organ is by Hill and Sons. The vicar is the Hon. E. Carr-Glyn.

ST. MARY ABBOTT, KENSINGTON.

ST. MARY ABBOTT, KENSINGTON.

ST. MARY'S, PIMLICO.

ST. MARY'S is another church built within the last few years, and is a good example of the time at which it was built. Its architect was Mr. Withers; the style, that of the thirteenth century. It holds 400 persons. The organ is by Walker. The curate-in-charge is the Rev. R. Eyton.

Plate 25

Church of St Mary the Virgin,
Graham Street, Pimlico, S.W.
Erected 1874.

Plate 26

Church of St Mary the Virgin,
Graham Street, Pimlico, S.W.

ST. JUDE'S, SOUTH KENSINGTON.

IN St. Jude's Church, of which the vicar is the Rev. R. W. Forrest, we are recalled by the architects—Messrs. George and Henry Godwin[1] —to the style of a somewhat earlier period in London church building. They have here successfully met the three special demands of the day—moderation in cost, the use of iron in conjunction with wood and stone, with the utmost practical absence of obstruction to the seeing of the officiating clergyman by the whole congregation. It has been lately finished and richly decorated, and seats as many as 1,700 persons. The organ is by Wedlake.

[1] To Mr. George Godwin, who has for so many years been known to the architectural world as the editor of the *Builder*, we are indebted for material assistance in obtaining several of the engravings in the present work. Many years ago he himself published a work on the 'Churches of London,' containing a large amount of valuable information and numerous illustrations.

ST. JUDE, SOUTH KENSINGTON.

ST. JUDE'S, KENSAL GREEN.

St. Jude's Church, of which the vicar is the Rev. S. Bott, was raised as a memorial church to the late Mr. Shaw, at a cost of £6,500. We give views of the interior and exterior. Its architect was Mr. J. T. Lee. It seats 800 persons.

CHURCH AND SCHOOL-HOUSE OF ST JUDE, KENSAL GREEN.

ST. CHAD'S, HAGGERSTON.

ST. CHAD'S, of which the vicar is the Rev. W. R. Sharpe, is a characteristic example of the church architecture of the date of its erection—1869—when the zeal for church building was perhaps at its highest. Its architect was Mr. J. Brooks. It seats 800 persons. Our engraving shows that part of the building known as the 'Morning Chapel.' The organ is by Walker.

ST. AUGUSTINE'S, KILBURN.[1]

THE Rev. R. C. Kirkpatrick is the vicar of St. Augustine's. It is a costly church, designed by Mr. Pearson, and, in some respects, on a plan unlike that of any other existing church; vaulted with stone throughout, and with a species of gallery or triforium, designed for processions. In matters of architectural decoration it is simple, and seats 1,600 persons. The organ is by Willis.

[1] Our engraving is photo-lithographed from a photograph of Mr. Samuel Walker, of Regent Street.

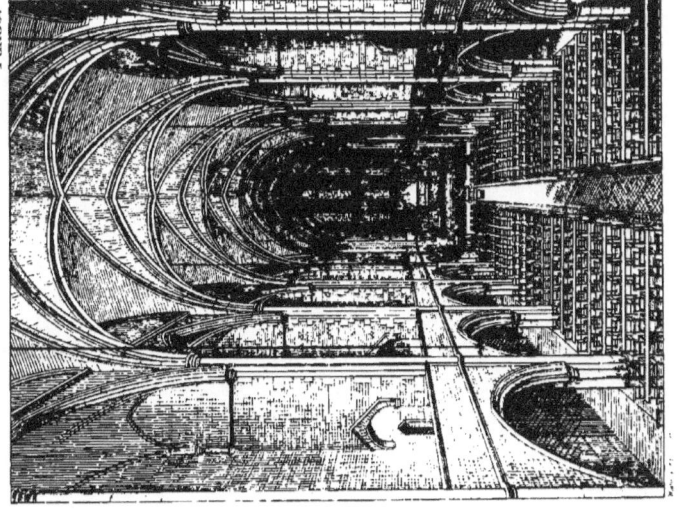

ST AUGUSTINE, KILBURN.

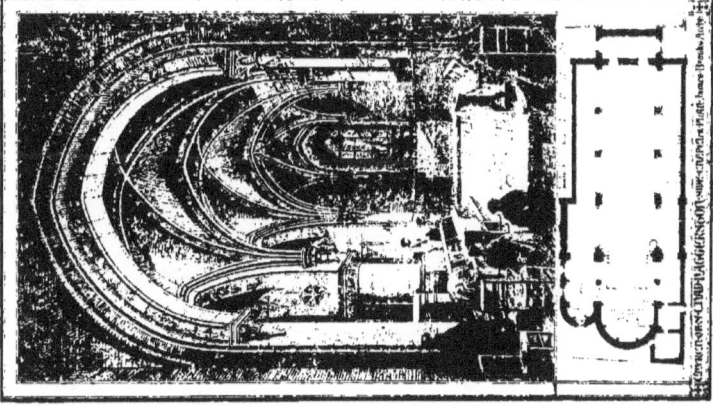

ST. MARY'S, STOKE NEWINGTON.

ST. MARY'S CHURCH, of which the Rev. T. Jackson is the rector, takes us back to an early period of Sir Gilbert Scott's church-building history. It is a large building, holding 1,300 persons; and it is interesting to compare it with his design for St. Giles's, Camberwell, built some years before. St. Mary's was built in 1858. The organ is by Gray and Davison.

ST. JAMES-THE-LESS, WESTMINSTER.

THE Rev. G. D. W. Dickson is the vicar of St. James-the-Less. It is a memorial church, built by the daughters of Bishop Monk, of Gloucester, in 1861. Its architect was Mr. Street. It holds 600 persons. The organ is by Nicholson, of Worcester.

ST. MARY, STOKE-NEWINGTON.

PLATE 33.   ST. JAMES-THE-LESS, WESTMINSTER.

ST. SAVIOUR'S, OXFORD STREET.

ST. SAVIOUR'S is a church with a special interest of its own, being designed for the use of the deaf and dumb; and also as showing the ingenuity with which its architect, Mr. Arthur Blomfield, has adapted the arrangement of its ground plan to the peculiar character of the services for which it is designed: notwithstanding its confined situation, the building includes convenient accommodation for the chaplain, the Rev. S. Smith, and for its numerous inmates; while underneath the church itself is a spacious lecture hall. It holds 250 persons.

PLATE 34.   ST. SAVIOUR, OXFORD STREET.

ST. GABRIEL'S, PIMLICO.

ST. GABRIEL'S, of which the Rev. B. Belcher is the vicar, takes us back to an early date in the church-building movement. It is a large church, built by Mr. T. Cundy, in the style of the fourteenth century, holding about 1,100 persons. In a chamber at the end of the North Aisle is a fine organ, built by Bevington and Sons, of Soho, London, in 1854, from a specification of the late J. B. Brownsmith, Vicar Choral of Westminster Abbey, who was organist and director of the choir in this church for some years. The instrument contains three manuals and pedal organ, forty stops, six couplers, and 1,800 pipes.

ST. JOHN BAPTIST'S, KENSINGTON.

ST. JOHN BAPTIST'S CHURCH, of which the vicar is the Rev. G. Booker, is an example of what can really be done by the architects of to-day —in this case Mr. J. Brooks—where the architect is not hampered by narrowness of site or deficiency in funds. It seats 878. The organ is by Gern.

Plate 35

Plate 36

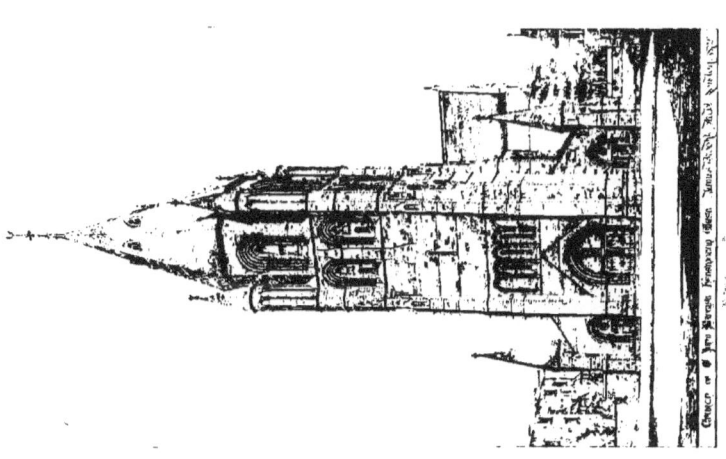

NEW CHURCH OF ST GABRIEL, WARWICK-SQUARE, PIMLICO

Advertisements connected with the Decoration and Completion of Old and New Churches.

SHRIGLEY & HUNT

ART WORKERS IN

STAINED GLASS

MURAL DECORATIONS

TILES · MOSAICS

AND

MEMORIAL BRASSES

JOHN O'GAUNT'S GATE · LANCASTER

AND

28 JOHN STREET · BEDFORD ROW

LONDON · W.C.

ESTABLISHED PRIOR TO 1750.

A CLERGYMAN writes, respecting a preparation for the brain and nerves, prepared according to Dr. PERCY's Formula: 'I could not write my sermons or feel interested in my duties. My physician ordered me to take *Vitalized Phosphates*. I obtained it from the druggist. I have taken it but a week and am feeling much better; my memory is restored; I can think and write as usual; my dyspeptic troubles are gone, and I sleep well. It is called a *Brain and Nerve Food*. It has been both to me.'

Physicians alone have prescribed 157,780 bottles of 'Vitalized Phosphates' as pleasant to take and FREE FROM ALL DANGER.

Sold by every Chemist, price **3/9** *per bottle (containing 44 adult doses), or POST FREE from* F. CROSBY, 137A Strand, London, *upon receipt of Stamps or P.O.O.*

Send for a descriptive pamphlet, containing high-class Testimonials, which will be sent to you post free. It is well worth reading.

THOMAS PRATT & SONS,

Clerical Tailors, Hatters, Robe, Cassock, Surplice, & Vestment Makers,

CATALOGUES OF CLERICAL CLOTHING, CHURCH FURNITURE, CHURCH PLATE, CASSOCKS, SURPLICES, CLERICAL HATS, STAINED GLASS, ALTAR CLOTHS, &c. &c.
SENT FREE ON APPLICATION.

Makers of the Improved Episcopal Robes, worn by the Bishops of Lincoln, Truro, and Durham, and supplied to many Colonial and American Bishops.

ORIGINAL INVENTORS OF THE POCKET SURPLICE.

In Black Leather Case, sent on receipt of Post Office Order for 21s., payable at Charing Cross. EXTRA LENGTH, to wear without Cassock, 26s.

☞ MANY THOUSANDS OF THESE SURPLICES ARE AT PRESENT IN USE.

ECCLESIASTICAL SHOW ROOMS:
23 & 24 TAVISTOCK STREET (NEAR COVENT GARDEN), & 14 SOUTHAMPTON STREET, STRAND, LONDON, W.C.

JONES & WILLIS

ART-WORKERS IN METAL AND WOOD WORK FOR ECCLESIASTICAL & DOMESTIC PURPOSES.

COMMUNION PLATE, COMPLETE SETS, FROM 60s.

CORONAS, STANDARDS, GASALIERS, GRILLS, GRATES, BRACKETS, VASES, CANDLESTICKS, LECTERNS, MEMORIAL BRASSES, TOMB RAILINGS, &c. &c. PULPITS, ALTARS, CHAIRS, STANDS, DESKS, LECTERN SEATS, SCREENS, REREDOS, ALMS BOXES, &c.

Manufacturers and Patentees of the Hesperus Star Lamp, equal to 45 Candles.

MANUFACTURERS OF TEXTILE FABRICS.

Embroidery, Carpets, Damasks, Hassocks, Velvets, Cloths, Fringes, Laces, Linen Cloths, &c.

STAINED GLASS.   STONE CARVERS.

Catalogues, containing **1,400** Woodcuts and Special Designs, free on application.
ARCHITECTS' DESIGNS CARRIED OUT AND ESTIMATES GIVEN.

BIRMINGHAM—TEMPLE ROW.
LONDON—Show Rooms, 43 GREAT RUSSELL STREET, W.C.
Works, 206 EUSTON ROAD, N.W.

A SHORT ACCOUNT OF THE REED ORGAN.

AS the whistle has been slowly developed into an organ pipe, and by experimental changes in the shape and size of this simple instrument the immense power and variety of the great organ has been evolved, so from the vibration of a piece of metal the reed organ, with its comparatively simple mechanism and its pleasing harmony, has been produced. Attempts to combine these two original sources of musical sound in anything like equal proportions have thus far been unsuccessful, at least for any practical purpose, since they are differently affected by atmospheric influences, and exhibit a constant tendency to divergence in tone. In the great organ a few sets of reeds are used, but it requires the constant care of the organist to keep the pipes in accord with them.

When the tuning-fork is struck the tone is not perceived except close to the ear, since the pulsations of the air caused by the vibrations of the steel are slight, and reach but a little distance. The coarser and less musical sounds of the jewsharp are heard farther because they come out with a moving current of air. This fact probably gave the hint for the expedient adopted in the reed organ, which is to place the reed in a current of air put in motion by means of a bellows. The term 'reed' is derived from the slip of real reed bound upon the mouthpiece of the clarinet and similar instruments, by means of which a peculiar vibration is imparted to the air that is blown through the tube. In an organ the 'reed' is a metal tongue, or vibrator, generally of brass, fixed in a metallic block, and exactly fitting a slit made for it. The comparative length, width, and thickness of the vibrator will determine the pitch of the sound it gives out, since all the notes of a musical scale have an invariable correspondence in the number of vibrations per second. These reeds in their general form are struck out and the parts rivetted by machinery; but it is at this point that the real difficulty begins. Long and patient experiments have led the musical artisan to results that cannot be well explained except at the workman's bench. The reed is carefully manipulated so as to produce the desired tone. Certainly four or more distinct qualities of tone can be made by the different mode of finishing the same piece of brass. This process is called 'voicing,' and is wholly distinct from the business of tuning. The tuner regards the pitch solely, and with a delicate file he takes off an imperceptible bit of length, to make vibration quicker, and therefore to produce a tone a trifle sharper; or he makes the reed a trifle thinner, which retards the rate of vibration and makes the tone flat. These reeds, when voiced and tuned, are set in a tube-board, which has the proper number of perforations, called reed-cells; also air passages from each cell leading into the 'receiver,' or under part of the bellows. In the AMERICAN ORGAN this tube-board, with its cells of reeds, forms the top of an air-tight box, in which the vibration takes place, thereby producing a much fuller and more

musical resonance. From this space, termed the resonant air chamber, a channel leads into the 'receiver.' The bellows, when acted upon by treadles, is alternately distended and released, causing an exhaustion of the air in the 'receiver,' and consequently a steady current through the reeds downward. In the Alexandre Organs this process is reversed, the bellows pressing the air upwards through the reeds. By pressure the reeds give out a louder tone, but it is far less agreeable to musical ears than that produced by an exhausting bellows. The player puts the bellows in motion, and draws the stop which lets in the air to the desired register; then, when he touches a key, a pin below it opens the valve under its proper reed; the air in its motion sets the metallic tongue vibrating, and we hear the organ tone. But as good taste requires light and shade, and the ear is fatigued by a tone of monotonous force, a 'swell' is provided. This is a softly-padded door that closes over the cells, and keeps the tone in check, muffled as it were, until it is the pleasure of the organist to let out its full power. The motion of the swell is governed by pressure from the knee. Much of the same sort of effect is produced also by the manner of blowing— an art that one must acquire by experience, and which is difficult to describe. The office of the stop marked *Forte* is to open the swell to the full extent, and so give the maximum power. By the *Tremolo* a mechanical wave is communicated to the current of air—a pleasing effect if sparingly used. In large instruments all of these elements are variously combined for effects. For instance, when there are two manuals or keyboards, they may be united by a *Manual Coupler*, so that touching one key operates corresponding notes in each. There is also an *Octave Coupler*, by which one key sounds its own proper note and its octave at the same time. Pedals give the fundamental harmony, and can also be connected to the registers of the manuals by a *Pedal Coupler*, and so give a delicate accompaniment when it is wanted. In the large organs the blowing is done by an assistant, the player using the treadle only in soft passages.

A compact, strong, and smoothly-finished piece of cabinet work encloses the whole. It will be seen that, though the conception of the reed organ is a simple one, many things are necessary to its success *as a work of art*. The work of cabinet-makers, brass-finishers, bellows-makers, and varnishers is, of course, wholly mechanical. In every conceivable way the power of machinery is used to lighten labour and to expedite results. Many parts of the organ are made far more swiftly and unerringly by machinery than they could be by the best workmen. But there is something beyond all this; and that which is most vital to a musical instrument comes from the refined taste, the sharpened faculties, the long experience, and the unwearied attention of the men who devote their lives to the art.

Readers are invited to call at the Organ Saloon of the Sunday School Union, 56 Old Bailey, London, E.C., and inspect these Magnificent Instruments.

ILLUSTRATED CATALOGUES AND PRICES FOR CASH OR ON THE THREE YEARS' SYSTEM UPON APPLICATION TO THE TRADE MANAGER,

56 OLD BAILEY, LONDON, E.C.

BEVINGTON & SONS,
ORGAN BUILDERS,

First Class Medals.
Paris, 1855.
London, 1862.
Paris, 1867.

ROSE STREET, SOHO, LONDON, W.

DESIGNERS AND BUILDERS
OF ALL KINDS OF

CHURCH, SALOON, AND CHAMBER ORGANS.

Price Lists, and every information respecting Repairs, Additions, and Tunings, given on application.

The following is a List of some of the important Organs, public and private, built by BEVINGTON & SONS:

- CHAPEL of the FOUNDLING HOSPITAL, London.
- St. MARTIN'S-IN-THE-FIELDS, London.
- St. GABRIEL'S, Pimlico, ,,
- St. PAUL'S, Covent Garden, ,,
- CHRIST CHURCH, Mayfair, ,,
- St. MARY'S, Bryanstone Square, ,,
- St. SAVIOUR'S, Haverstock Hill, ,,
- St. ANN'S, South Lambeth, ,,
- MASONIC HALL, Golden Square ,,
- ALL SAINTS', Finchley Road, ,,
- PARK CHAPEL, Chelsea, ,,
- St. JOHN'S CHURCH, Kilburn, ,,
- St. GEORGE'S GARRISON CHURCH, Woolwich.
- ALL SAINTS' CHURCH, Southampton.
- QUEEN STREET CHAPEL, Wolverhampton.
- St. SAVIOUR'S CHURCH, Hampstead.
- AIGBURTH CHURCH, near Liverpool.
- WRANGTHORNE CHURCH, Leeds.
- ROYAL MILITARY COLLEGE, Sandhurst.
- St. JAMES'S CHURCH, Rochdale.
- St. ANN'S CHURCH, Lancaster.
- WELLINGTON CHURCH, Salop.
- HOLY TRINITY CHURCH, Tulse Hill.
- St. PAUL'S CHURCH, Birmingham.
- St. NICHOLAS' CHURCH, Newbury.
- St. MARY'S CHURCH, Brighton.
- SLAIDBURN CHURCH Clitheroe.
- St. PATRICK'S CATHEDRAL, Dublin.
- R. C. CATHEDRAL, Carlow.
- R. C. CATHEDRAL, Tuam.
- R. C. CATHEDRAL, Longford.
- R. C. CHURCH, Cashel.
- St. CANICE CATHEDRAL, Kilkenny.
- R. C. CATHEDRAL, Sydney, N.S.W.
- QUEBEC CATHEDRAL.
- St. GEORGE'S CATHEDRAL, Cape.
- St. GEORGE'S CATHEDRAL, Grahamstown.
- R. C. CATHEDRAL, Costa Rica.
- St. MATTHEW'S CHURCH, Dunedin, N.Z.
- PRO-CATHEDRAL, Rangoon, British Burmah.
- First PRESBYTERIAN CHURCH, Oakland, California.
- HOLY TRINITY CHURCH, Cannes.
- CHURCH OF THE RESURRECTION, Brussels.
- R. C. CATHEDRAL, Honolulu, Sandwich Islands.

CHAMBER ORGANS.

CHARLES VENABLES, Esq., Taplow; 3 Manuals and Pedal; blown by water.
J. A. ROLLS, Esq., The Hendre, Monmouth; 2 Manuals and Pedal; blown by water.
T. CORDES, Esq., M.P., Bryn Glas, Newport, Mon.; 1 Manual;

Sir WILLIAM MUIR, Kensington; 2 Manuals; blown by water.
Rev. C. HARRIS, Tooting; 2 Manuals.
G. M. SMITH, Esq., Elmhurst, Clapham; 2 Manuals and Pedals blown by water.
JOHN LYSAGHT, Esq., Stoke Bishop; 3 Manuals and Pedal; blown by gas engine.

THE

CAMPBELL BRICK AND TILE COMPANY,

STOKE-UPON-TRENT.

ENCAUSTIC, MAJOLICA,

AND

GEOMETRICAL TILES

AND

MOSAICS,

For Churches, Public Buildings, Halls, Conservatories, Hearths, Fireplaces, Baths, Walls, &c.

LONDON WAREHOUSE AND SHOW ROOM:
206 GREAT PORTLAND STREET, W.

DESIGNS AND ESTIMATES FREE ON APPLICATION.

HARLAND & FISHER,
33 SOUTHAMPTON STREET, STRAND, W.C.
ART DECORATORS.

CHURCH AND DOMESTIC DECORATION, PAINTED MAJOLICA TILES, EMBROIDERY PAPER HANGINGS, AND ART FURNITURE.
CHURCH DECORATION OF EVERY DESCRIPTION, STAINED AND PAINTED WINDOWS FOR CHURCHES AND DWELLINGS.
MURAL PAINTINGS IN OIL, ENCAUSTIC, AND TEMPERA.
GLASS AND MARBLE MOSAIC, MAJOLICA PAINTING ON TILES FOR FIGURE AND ORNAMENTAL WORK, AS PERMANENT AS MOSAIC, AT LESS THAN ONE-THIRD THE PRICE.
DESIGNERS AND MANUFACTURERS OF DOMESTIC ART FURNITURE AND NEEDLEWORK FOR CURTAINS, HANGINGS, &c., ALSO ALTAR CLOTHS AND CHURCH EMBROIDERY.
MEDIÆVAL, QUEEN ANNE, AND OTHER PAPER HANGINGS.
DESIGNERS AND ENGRAVERS OF MONUMENTAL BRASSES, &c.
Designs and Estimates furnished for the Complete Decoration of Public and Private Buildings in any part of the Country.

ESTABLISHED 1755.
WM. HILL & SON,
ORGAN BUILDERS,
YORK ROAD, CAMDEN ROAD, LONDON, N.

BUILDERS OF THE ORGANS IN THE FOLLOWING CATHEDRALS, &c.

York Minster (Great Screen Organ and Nave Organ), Worcester (Great Transept Organ and Choir ditto), Chichester, Ely, Peterboro', Manchester, St. Asaph, Bangor, St. Albans, Westminster Abbey; Town Hall, Birmingham; Ulster Hall, Belfast; Music Hall, Edinburgh University; Town Hall, Melbourne, Australia; Town Hall, Adelaide, Australia; H.M. Chapels Royal, St. James, Whitehall, Buckingham Palace, Windsor.

COLLEGE CHAPELS.
CAMBRIDGE:—Trinity, St. John's, King's, University Church, Pembroke, Christ's, Emmanuel, Catherine's, Peterhouse. OXFORD:—Brasenose, Exeter, Corpus Christi, &c., &c.

ESTABLISHED 1740. ## THWAITES & REED, ESTABLISHED 1740.
15 BOWLING GREEN LANE (LATE OF ROSOMAN STREET), CLERKENWELL, LONDON, E.C.

MANUFACTURERS FOR HOME AND EXPORT OF

CHURCH,
TURRET,
STABLE,

AND OTHER
CLOCKS
OF
ALL DESCRIPTIONS,
With Compensated & other Pendulums, of the Best Materials and Workmanship; also
RINGING AND CHIMING MACHINES,
Playing any number of Tunes.

ESTIMATES FREE ON APPLICATION.
By the erection of New and Improved Machinery, driven by gas power, THWAITES and REED are enabled to execute all orders at short notice, and at the lowest possible prices.

ABERDEEN POLISHED GRANITE MONUMENTS,
FROM £5.
LETTER-CUTTING ACCURATE AND BEAUTIFUL.
BEST QUALITY GRANITE AND MARBLE WORK OF ALL KINDS.
IRON RAILINGS AND TOMB FURNISHINGS FITTED COMPLETE.
PLANS, PRICES, AND CARRIAGE-FREE TERMS TO ALL PARTS OF THE WORLD, FROM

J. W. LEGGE, Sculptor,
ABERDEEN, SCOTLAND.

J. WESTELL'S
LIST OF ARCHITECTURAL AND OTHER WORKS
AT REDUCED PRICES.
549 NEW OXFORD STREET, LONDON.

LIBRARIES AND PARCELS OF MISCELLANEOUS AND THEOLOGICAL BOOKS PURCHASED.

STANDARD WORK ON ECCLESIASTICAL ORNAMENT.

PUGIN'S GLOSSARY OF ECCLESIASTICAL ORNAMENT AND COSTUME. Setting forth the Origin, History, and Mystical Signification of the various Emblems, Devices, and Symbolical Colours, peculiar to CHRISTIAN DESIGN of the MIDDLE AGES, with especial reference to the DECORATION of the SACRED VESTMENTS and ALTAR FURNITURE formerly used in the English Church. Illustrated by 73 Plates, *all specially printed in* Gold and Colours, *by the Lithochromotographic process, and about 50 Woodcuts in the Letter-press. Third Edition.* 1 vol. imperial 4to. sells at £7. 7s.; *elegantly half-bound in red morocco, gilt top, uncut*, £4. 1868
The same, wanting 1 Plate, 4to, morocco, £2. 2s. 1844

BRANDON (R. & J. A.) PARISH CHURCHES; being Perspective Views of English Ecclesiastical Structures. With Plans and Letter-press. Royal 8vo. many Plates, half-calf, neat, £1. 1s. 1848

BOUTELL (C.) MONUMENTAL BRASSES AND SLABS OF THE MIDDLE AGES. Many Plates and Cuts. Royal 8vo. cloth, 15s. 1848

HAINES' (H.) MANUAL OF MONUMENTAL BRASSES AND LIST OF THOSE REMAINING IN THE BRITISH ISLES. 200 Plates. 2 vols. 8vo. cloth, scarce, 17s. 1861

FOSBROKE (T. D.) BRITISH MONACHISM, OR MANNERS AND CUSTOMS OF THE MONKS AND NUNS OF ENGLAND. Plates. Royal 8vo. cloth, 12s. 1843

WILLIS (R.) ON THE ARCHITECTURE OF THE MIDDLE AGES. 15 Plates. Royal 8vo. cloth, large paper, 5s. 1835

THEOPHILUS (PRIEST AND MONK) ON THE ARTS OF THE MIDDLE AGES. Translated, with Notes, by R. HENDRIE. Facsimile, Latin and English. 8vo. cloth, 7s. 1847

POOLE (G. A.) HISTORY OF ECCLESIASTICAL ARCHITECTURE IN ENGLAND. Portrait of INIGO JONES. 8vo. cloth, 4s. 1848

BRAYLEY & BRITTON'S HISTORY OF THE ANCIENT PALACE AND LATE HOUSES OF PARLIAMENT. Plates. Royal 8vo. cloth, large paper, 6s. 6d. 1836

SHARP (E.) ON THE RISE AND PROGRESS OF DECORATED WINDOW TRACERY IN ENGLAND. Many Plates. 2 vols. 8vo. cloth, scarce, 18s. 1849

HULL (E.) ON THE BUILDING AND ORNAMENTAL STONES OF GREAT BRITAIN AND FOREIGN COUNTRIES. Plates. 8vo. cloth, 7s. 6d. 1872

PIRANESÉ (G. B.) DE ROMANORUM MAGNIFICENTIA ET ARCHITECTURA. 44 fine large Plates and Portrait. Royal folio, half-morocco, fine copy, £2. 2s. Roma, 1761

BARTOLI COLONNA TRAJANI. 119 fine Plates. Oblong folio, red morocco, gilt edges, a fine copy, £1. 15s. Roma, 1690

BARTOLI ROMANARUM ANTIQUITATUM VESTIGIA. Oblong folio. 84 fine Plates, half-calf, gilt, 18s. Roma, 1693

J. WESTELL, English & Foreign Bookseller, 549 New Oxford Street, London.

A CLERGYMAN writes, respecting a preparation for the brain and nerves, prepared according to Dr. PERCY'S Formula: 'I could not write my sermons or feel interested in my duties. My physician ordered me to take *Vitalized Phosphates*. I obtained it from the druggist. I have taken it but a week and am feeling much better; my memory is restored; I can think and write as usual; my dyspeptic troubles are gone, and I sleep well. It is called a *Brain and Nerve Food*. It has been both to me.'

Physicians alone have prescribed 157,780 bottles of 'Vitalized Phosphates' as pleasant to take and FREE FROM ALL DANGER.

Sold by every Chemist, price **3/9** *per bottle (containing 44 adult doses), or POST FREE from* F. CROSBY, 137A Strand, London, *upon receipt of Stamps or P.O.O.*

Send for a descriptive pamphlet, containing high-class Testimonials, which will be sent to you post free. It is well worth reading.

www.ingramcontent.com/pod-product-compliance
Lightning Source LLC
Chambersburg PA
CBHW021945160426
43195CB00011B/1231